Few times of wander

Tien Thuy Quach

Presentation by *BookLeaf Publishing*

Web: www.bookleafpub.com

E-mail: info@bookleafpub.com

ISBN: 9789357211048

First edition 2022

DEDICATION

Dedicate to those who were and would be in the middle of the loss of someone or something that they have been treasured (especially due to the Covid-19 pandemic)!

Dedicate to those who continuously love and care about ourselves, even though we sometimes forget about their existence!

Dedicate to those who are not the strongest, but are the most trying to move forward in a strange place or at a new time!

ACKNOWLEDGEMENT

I would like to express my deep appreciation to my family, teachers, friends, and other colleagues for their outstanding love and support throughout my whole life. Without their understanding and encouragement, I couldn't become "myself" today and had a chance to complete this book!

This book is in honour of my beloved people, particularly great grandma Lê Thị Nội, dear friend Nguyễn Thị Xuân Ngọc, and strong colleague Nguyễn Hữu Phước.
You are always loved and forever in our hearts!

PREFACE

Hi everyone,

I am Tien and it's my pleasure to participate in the 29-days Poem Challenge (April 2022) which was the origin of this book.

I would like to briefly share with you my thoughts when living in the United Kingdom. It's totally ok for "few times of wander" so we don't need to hide or neglect them. Let me know if you somehow feel the same!

I understand that my knowledge and skills are limited compared to others, but I hope some of you can be empowered to pursue your own belief and passion after reading my book. Your comments and feedback are valuable to improve my writing, so please feel free to contact me via LinkedIn (https://www.linkedin.com/in/tien-thuy-quach/).

Thank you!

Tien

GLOW

Grace might come from the meadow
Lustre might be found in the super-show
Operators had already made it on-flow
Warmth would raise with the rainbow

GLASGOW

Glory might shine on the hollow
Lark might pass across the pillow
Assets might fly out the window
Soul might be covered by shadow
Gloss might be over the shallow
One might endure the heavy snow
Wisdom could bring back our tomorrow

ENJOY

3

Earth might bury under the umbra
Navigation might go around the libra
Journey might happen as the opera
Once we kept holding the penumbra
You could wrongly open the Pandora

EDINBURGH

Ecstasy might flood over the boroughs
Innocents might remain as the labra
Nobles might fall on the zebra
Believers might look for the sutra
Understanding could sway all the spectra
Receivers could trade off the sera
Givers could spread out the aura
Humans could create the new era

NEED

5

New-borns might belong to certain camps
Experimenters might carry out the exams
Entrepreneurs might pull down the dams
Defenders must stand over the slam

NOTTINGHAM

Natives might familiarise with the anagrams
Originators might be our great grandams
Travelers might ultilise the modern webcams
Tenders might alert the ordinary spam
Initiators could launch the new epigrams
Narrators could follow the Great Cham
Governors could promote the fundraising
programs
Helpers could explain the block diagrams
Adapters could follow the proposed RAM
Motivators could lighten all the lamps

LOOK

Learners might want the guidons
Offspring might protect the tendons
Olympians might restrict the abandon
Keepers should free the guerdons

LONDON

Leaders could trust the myrmidons
Overseers could want the celadons
Nominators could play the bombardon
Directors could ring the bourdons
Organisers could give the pardons
Nations would assure the Dons

LIGHT

Loneliness might come from the festers
Ingenuity might come from the dopesters
Goodness might come from the presters
Humour might come from the jesters
Trust could come from the rosters

LEICESTER

Liveliness might come from the jokesters
Enthusiasm might come from the contesters
Inspiration might come from the testers
Courage might come from the wresters
Encouragement might come from the suggesters
Self-esteem might come from the nesters
Thankfulness might come from the attesters
Exclusive might come from the protesters
Rationale could come from the questers

MARVEL

Makers might grow northwester
Assigners might be sequestered
Runners might be festered
Vaunters might be watered
Enchanters might be pestered
Lovers should stay southwester

MANCHESTER

Managers might become masters
Assisters might support darters
Nomenclators might get voters
Carers might contact venters
Handlers might chase costers
Entertainers might bring titter
Suppliers might buy pasters
Teachers might require paters
Employers might write jotters
Relievers could stop wasters

LIKE

13

Lords could have the tools
Infants might play the pools
Kingpins might become the fools
Epicureans might enjoy the cool

LIVERPOOL

Libertarians could cut the spools
Inheritors could have the drool
Valedictorians could be found at schools
Experts could examine the toadstools
Regulators could control the preschool
Pacificists could turn into supercool
Optimists could come out tomfools
Officers could purify the cesspools
Literate could enhance the interschool

BOUND

Balance might usually exist in mast
Offers might sometimes go very fast
Utmost might truly express at last
Nature might always hide the vast
Devotion might possibly improve our past

BELFAST

Beauty might correspond to the gymnasts
Equality might maintain among the dicasts
Legislation might not use the bombast
Freedom might not only be bypast
Amity might strongly avoid the miscast
Sufficiency might consider for the outcasts
Transparency could ease off the contrast

BLESS

Benefaction might be remembered as ideograms
Luxury might increase due to telegrams
Efficiency might build up the kymograms
Savvy might be given to madams
Serenity could be observed from phenogams

BIRMINGHAM

Bravery might need for the tomograms
Intelligence might lead to the wolfram
Renovation might result in the venograms
Movement might expand through the trams
Independence might enhance the holograms
Nicety could cover up the ginghams
Generosity could be hidden from logograms
Harmony could be kept under Schiedam
Authority could support flotsam and jetsam
Majesty would be Mary and William

BOOST

Brevity of life might be pistoled
Objectives of study could explain amatol
Opportunities for work were from capitol
Sensibility of peace was under santol
Tranquillity of mind maintained by eucalyptol

BRISTOL

Backbones of network steady as sorbitol
Recovery of health important as ethambutol
Ideas of help necessary as mannitol
Significance of test relevant to polyols
Taste of success sweet as xylitol
Oodles of love spread out Bristol
Lust for happiness would be extolled

WANDER

Walk as the voyagers
Accelerate as the strangers
Neutralise as the bonders
Decide as the advisers
Enrich as the nurturers
Reward as the treasurers